How to Avoid Conflicts BEFORE Your Class is Disrupted

Understanding Learning Styles and Discipline

Rosemary Dolinsky

How to Avoid Conflicts BEFORE Your Class is Disrupted

Copyright © 2009 by Rosemary Dolinsky

All rights reserved. No part of this book may be reproduced or transmitted in any form or by any means without written permission of the author.

This book is dedicated to all the wonderful educators
who believe it is non-negotiable to leave no child behind!

Table of Contents

How to Avoid Conflicts BEFORE Your Class is Disrupted
Understanding Learning Styles and Discipline

Rosemary Dolinsky

Identifying Styles 1

Discipline Problems and How to Avoid Them 15

Creating Classroom Expectations 25

Following Classroom Expectations 33

Choosing Consequences 39

Postscript 47

Identifying Styles
_____

1

Identifying Styles

Everyone learns in different ways. Just as we like different types of music, have different friends or wear different clothing, we also prefer learning in different ways. As an educator, it is essential for you to understand your students learning styles since not only do learning styles determine your students ability to learn your objectives easily and effectively, but to understand they influence how your student behaves in your classroom and responds to your discipline methods.

A personal learning style is nothing short of a sensory preference. Your senses take in approximately 50000 impressions every second. This is such as extraordinary about of information...far too much for

Identifying Styles

your brain to deal with consciously. Because of this stimuli overload, your brain focuses primarily on one or two senses. Students develop a preference over time for one sense over another to gather and process information from their environment. In other words, they lean on one particular sense to represent most, but not all of their sensory experience.

To understand how each of your students prefers to learn, it is NOT necessary for you to give them the formal written assessment that I have included in this section. All you need to do is to LISTEN to your students when they speak and OBSERVE their behaviors.

LISTEN TO YOUR STUDENTS' VOCABULARY

Each style has its own distinct vocabulary. Since we tend to use language that connects with our style, vocabulary gives you a real starting point for determining whether your student is:

(1) Auditory learner who learns best by listening, reading aloud and talking; or
(2) Visual learner who learns best by watching, visualizing or drawing, or
(3) Kinesthetic learner who learns best by doing and moving.

You can ascertain the differences by listening to the vocabulary that your student uses.

How to Avoid Conflicts BEFORE Your Class is Disrupted

 THE VISUALS

Students, who rely on seeing, the Visuals, use "picture" words such as:
- I can VISUALIZE it.
- I can PICTURE it.
- I can SEE that.
- Let's FOCUS now.

 THE AUDITORIES

Students who rely on their auditory senses to learn, the Auditories, rely on "sound" vocabulary:

- TELL me.
- That's CLEAR as a BELL.
- Can you HEAR what I mean?
- Can we TALK?
- That SOUNDS right.

Identifying Styles

THE KINESTHETICS

Students who use movement as a means of learning, the Kinesthetics, may be heard using "moving" phrases:
- I'd like to GET a better idea of this information.
- I have a GUT feeling about this.
- Let's TOUCH BASE later.

OBSERVING THE AUDITORY LEARNER

Auditory learners HAVE DIFFICULTY with:

- Reading silently without any time to discuss the information during the reading session
- Following written directions
- Focusing on pictures
- Taking read and written only timed tests
- Having extended time periods of silence
- Concentrating when there are distracting sounds
- Not expressing emotions verbally

Auditory learners are AT EASE with:

- Speaking without a script
- Noticing different sounds in the surrounding area
- Remembering the names of people met (faces are forgotten easily)

- Working with languages and words
- Recognizing inflection shifts when others are talking

Auditory learners SOLVE PROBLEMS by:

- Discussing the pros and cons of the situation
- Discussing options that can be implemented
- Asking others what they would do in the same situation
- Verbalize different solutions until one sounds right
- Repeating the problem aloud while discussing different solutions

Auditory STUDY STRATEGIES:

- Uses mnemonics to help remember
- Repeats information or directions aloud
- May move lips during silent reading
- Listens to instrumental music while studying
- Interrupts readings to discuss content

OBSERVING THE VISUAL LEARNER

Visual learners HAVE DIFFICULTY with:

- Working with surrounding noise or movement
- Listening to lectures without visuals
- Working in areas that are colorless and without decorations

Identifying Styles

- Working in an environment with TOO much visual stimulations
- Dealing with a distracting physical appearance
- Concentrating when there are distracting sounds
- Beginning an activity or taking any action without seeing or reading the directions

Visual learners are AT EASE with:

- Recalling details and colors of what has been seen
- Spelling, proofreading
- Remembering the faces of people met (names are forgotten easily unless seen in print)
- Creating mental images
- Putting together outfits to wear
- Remembering how to go from one place to another after only one visit

Visual learners SOLVE PROBLEMS by:

- Listing problems
- Create graphic organizers for thought organization
- Use flow charts
- Visualizes the problem in the mind's eye with solutions to "see" the outcome

Visual learners' STUDY STRATEGIES:

- Reads for pleasure and relaxation
- Likes no noise when reading

- Reads quickly
- Learns spelling in configurations and not phonetically
- Creates pictures to represent information needed to be learned

OBSERVING THE KINESTHETIC LEARNER

Kinesthetic learners HAVE DIFFICULTY with:

- Interpreting communication that is non verbal
- Effectively using verbal skills
- Sitting still (tends to fidget and needs to move)
- Listening to lectures longer than 5 minutes
- Remembering what was heard or seen (can recall what was done)
- Doesn't use physical gestures or movement when expressing emotions
- Sticking to one activity for long periods of time (frequently needs change)
- Following written directions

Kinesthetic learners are AT EASE with:

- Doing hands on projects
- Running, dancing, swimming, jumping, etc.
- Participating in challenges and/or competitions
- Using large motor muscles

Identifying Styles

Kinesthetic learners SOLVE PROBLEMS by:

- Taking action
- Physically attacking problems
- Exploring through trial and error
- Look for solutions that require physical activity

Kinesthetic learners' STUDY STRATEGIES:

- Reading "How to" books
- Reading for specific information rather than for enjoyment or pleasure
- Reads brief articles or books
- Studies for short periods and then moves around
- Rather study lying down on the bed or floor if not allowed to walk around while studying
- Enjoys chewing gum while studying (satisfies a need to move)

LEARNING STYLE INVENTORY

Discipline problems seem to disappear when your students are engaged in learning. The best way to guarantee student engagement is to tailor instruction to target the experiences each style craves. It is imperative that you remember this... teachers tend to teach using strategies that are comfortable to their individual styles and it is difficult at times to understand why some students are not "getting it."

How to Avoid Conflicts BEFORE Your Class is Disrupted

Please move out of your comfort zone since your style may not be effective for some students in your classroom.

On the next page is a learning styles assessment. Take the following test. You can use this test to determine your preference. This assessment may also be used with your students.

Identifying Styles

WHAT KIND OF LEARNER ARE YOU?

Directions: Circle the items that describe you:

1. If I am learning how to do something new, I would rather:
   (A) Talk about it.
   (V) Read about it quietly.
   (K) Create something with my hands related to the topic.

2. While reading, I often:
   (V) See pictures in my mind of what I am reading.
   (A) Read out loud to understand the information.
   (K) Fidget while I am reading.

3. When I tell someone how to do something, I:
   (V) Like using pictures to explain the information.
   (A) Have no trouble explaining the directions orally.
   (K) Gesture with my hands as I am talking.

4. When I am unsure of a spelling word, I:
   (V) Write the word on paper to see if it looks right.
   (A) Spell it out loud to hear if it sounds right.
   (K) Write the word in the air before I write it on paper.

5. While doing a report, I:
   (V) Pay attention to how well spaced my letters and words look.
   (A) Say what I want to write out loud.
   (K) Push hard on my pen as I am writing.

6. If I am studying facts, I need to:
   (V) Write the facts down on paper.
   (A) Say the facts over and over again.
   (K) Count the facts with my fingers and I walk around as I recite them.

7. I like it when my teacher:
   (V) Uses the board, overhead projector or shows pictures during a lesson.
   (A) Talks using lots of expression in his voice.
   (K) Uses hands on activities.

8. I have trouble remembering when:
   (V) The room is messy or there are people moving around.
   (A) The room I am in is very noisy.
   (K) I have I must sit at my desk for any length of time.

9. When I solve math problems:
   (V) I using drawings to see the problem.
   (A) Talk myself through the steps.
   (K) Move objects or use my body to help me think.

10. When I am given instructions on how to put something together, I:
    (V) Look at the pictures and try to see where the parts fit.
    (A) Read the directions out loud and talk to myself as I put the parts together.

Identifying Styles

(K) Put the parts together without reading the directions and then read later.

11. When I have nothing to do, I:
    (V) Look around, stare, or read.
    (A) Like to listen to other people's conversations.
    (K) Walk around and touch things with my hands.

12. When I am giving an oral report, I:
    (V) Using am quick because I don't like talking.
    (A) Go into detail because I like to talk.
    (K) Use gestures and like to move around/shift my body while I am talking.

13. When someone is talking to me, I:
    (V) Try to see what she is saying in my mind.
    (A) Enjoy listening but want to interrupt and talk myself.
    (K) Becomes bored if the report gets too long and detailed.

14. When trying to remember a person's name, I remember:
    (V) The face but not the name.
    (A) The name but forgets the face.
    (K) Where or when I met or learned about the person but not the name or face.

15. When I take a test, I:
    (V) Can see my notes or information in my mind.
    (A) Can hear the teacher's lesson in my mind.

How to Avoid Conflicts BEFORE Your Class is Disrupted

(K) Can remember hands on assignment to recall the information.

Scoring Instructions: Add the number of responses for each letter and enter the total below. The area with the highest number of responses is probably the way you learn best.

Visual (I see)   Auditory (I hear)   Kinesthetic (I move)

V= _____
A= _____
K= _____

I am probably a/an _____ learner.

Discipline Problems and How to Avoid Them

2

Discipline Problems and How to Deal With Them

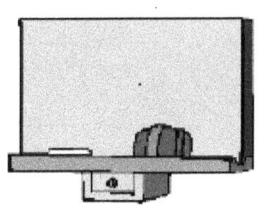 I would like you to close your eyes and visualize yourself standing in front of an imaginary chalkboard. Please list on that chalkboard the three learning styles. Next to each style, I would like you to doodle a picture that best depicts a characteristic of that style. (This is a great activity to "debrief" a learning episode for any objective you are teaching and hope the students remember.)

You should have listed auditory, visual and kinesthetic. A doodle next to the auditory may have been an ear, a radio or anything that had to do with hearing. Next to the visual, you may have drawn an eye, an artist palette, a magazine or anything else connected with seeing.

Discipline Problems and How to Avoid Them

Lastly, you may have drawn a runner, a baseball player, a skier or anything else to show movement.

Now that you have the learning styles down pat...let's move to discipline problem conflicts.

WHEN DISCIPLINE PROBLEMS ARISE

Often, there are discipline problems or conflicts when the teacher's learning style does not match the involved student. Sometimes a teacher's expectations about how a student "should" act really stems from personal and preferred learning styles. Does this mean you should disregard your style preference always in favor of your students? Absolutely not! It just means that sometimes your student learning needs will be a priority over your comfort zone. Also, just awareness of student frustrations and common misbehaviors can be enough to keep conflict at a minimal level.

The following story will help illustrate this point.

A fifth grade teacher I once observed was a very visual learner. Her classroom was quite neat and organized. She spoke using visual vocabulary..."picture this, do you see what I mean." One of her basic rules was all students were to stay in their seats unless they were instructed by her to leave them.

One day, she was teaching about different types of clouds. A very distinctive cloud formation was quite visible from the classroom window. During the lesson, she asked the students to "look" out the window at the sky. A few students, who I recognized immediately as

How to Avoid Conflicts BEFORE Your Class is Disrupted

a kinesthetic since I observed the fidgeting in their seats, got up to look at the mountain. This teacher thought these students were being rude and "breaking" her rule of remaining in their seats. Immediately, she had the students move back to their seats. Needless to say, looking at the clouds was "lost" since the lesson was interrupted by what the teacher misinterpreted as disrespect. It was after I talked to her about preferred learning styles did she simply realize the students were using their kinesthetic style which was to move. This teacher now understands the need for movement by some of her students. She told me whenever she wants her students to look at an object whether in the classroom or out the window, she now asks them all to get out their desks to "see" it. This strategy is out of her comfort zone, but quite effective since conflict has been eliminated.

Below are tables displaying common student frustrations and common teacher frustrations for individuals not using the same learning preference? It would be a good idea to print out these tables and leave them on your desk as a reminder of frustration differences.

COMMON STUDENT FRUSTRATION

	Kinesthetic Teacher	**Auditory Teacher**	**Visual Teacher**
Kinesthetic Student	Few frustrations This teaching style is a comfort zone for the kinesthetic student.	The kinesthetic student is frustrated by the teacher's emphasis on explaining and discussing rather than letting him do a hand's on activity.	The kinesthetic student is frustrated by the teacher always wanting him to read or look at pictures. Also, the student is frustrated by the low key classroom atmosphere.
Auditory Student	The auditory student is frustrated by not having verbal instructions with lots of details.	Few frustrations This teaching style is a comfort zone for the auditory student.	The auditory student is frustrated by the teacher wanting him to read or "look" at the directions to figure them out alone.
Visual Student	The visual student becomes overwhelmed by the kinesthetic teacher's level of energy	The visual student is constantly "talked to" by the auditory teacher.	Few frustrations This teaching style is a comfort zone for the visual student.

How to Avoid Conflicts BEFORE Your Class is Disrupted

COMMON TEACHER FRUSTRATION

	Kinesthetic Student	Auditory Student	Visual Student
Kinesthetic Teacher	Few frustrations This teaching style is a comfort zone for the kinesthetic teacher	The kinesthetic teacher is frustrated by the student's emphasis on talking.	The kinesthetic teacher is frustrated by the student always asking to see the information or asking for pictures.
Auditory Teacher	The auditory teacher is frustrated by student always asking to do something rather than sitting and listening.	Few frustrations This learning style is a comfort zone for the auditory teacher.	The auditory teacher is frustrated by the student who likes to draw, read or create mind maps rather than engage in conversation.
Visual Teacher	The visual teacher is frustrated and overwhelmed by the kinesthetic student's need to move.	The visual teacher is frustrated by the auditory student's constant need to talk and engage in discussion.	Few frustrations This learning style is a comfort zone for the visual teacher.

Discipline Problems and How to Avoid Them

MISBEHAVIORS

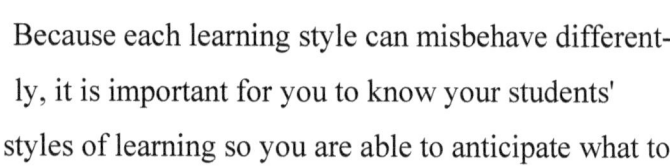

Because each learning style can misbehave differently, it is important for you to know your students' styles of learning so you are able to anticipate what to expect when a particular student is about to cause a conflict within your classroom.

So, let's talk about misbehaving tactics commonly used by different learning styles.

KINESTHETIC LEARNER MISBEHAVIORS

- Express discontent through body movement or gestures
- Often physically acts out
- Tends to create excitement from other students

AUDITORY LEARNER MISBEHAVIORS

- Often talks out of turn and does not listen
- Exchanges in verbal confrontations
- Often uses hurtful remarks or verbal attacks

VISUAL LEARNER MISBEHAVIORS

- Uses visual/nonverbal expressions
- Uses passive/aggressive behavior such as not talking to you
- May have unexpected outbursts from their built up silent treatment

TEACHER RESPONSES TO MISBEHAVIOR ACCORDING TO THEIR LEARNING STYLES

It is important for you to remember that the way you respond to a student is often determined by your preferred learning style. Even though is not your intention to isolate the student from you...that is exactly what you may end up doing if your discipline style does not match the student's.

Below are the preferred styles of discipline for the three different types of learners. Do you see yourself in anywhere?

- **Kinesthetic teachers** tend to use physical contact (such as a hand on the shoulder or standing in close proximity to the student)
- **Auditory teachers** tend to use reprimands and lectures when they discipline a student.
- **Visual teachers** tend to use body language such as "the look" or putting hands on hips. Also, visual teachers are the ones

who quickly isolate the student from the group by moving the student's desk.

How to Avoid Conflicts BEFORE Your Class is Disrupted

IDENTIFYING MISBEHAVIORS WORKSHEET

Use the following format to list on a separate sheet of paper five misbehaviors you encounter in your classroom on a regular basis. Using what you have learned about misbehaviors in this lesson, write next to the misbehavior associated with the learning style.

Misbehavior   Learning Style

1._____ _____

2._____ _____

3._____ _____

4._____ _____

5._____

When that is complete, answer the following questions:

Are most of the misbehaviors associated with a particular style?

What can you do to adjust to minimize the misbehavior?

Creating Classroom Expectations

3

Creating Classroom Expectations

I have always equated the word rule with negativity. Therefore, I am going to substitute the word rule in this lesson to "expectation." It is my personal opinion "expectation" is psychologically softer and does not give the impression of possible punishment. I do believe changing this word in the classroom will have a positive effect to your classroom management.

Students, like adults, are always asking "What's in it for me?" So, it is extremely important for you to take the time to communicate the purpose of your expectations and their consequences of not meeting them on a very personal level.

Take impersonality out of the expectation discussion and substitute it with ways the students can relate them to in their own lives.

Creating Classroom Expectations

For example, instead of just telling the students they must "apply effort to all work," ask them if they had any experiences when they did or did not work as well they could. Then, proceed to ask the consequences of that experience. List the consequences on the board. Connect that experience and consequences to your room.

Share your vision of what your classroom should look like and have your students to the same. By doing so, it makes for remembering and "following" the expectation in your room easier.

Guidelines for Creating and Implementing Expectations in Your Classroom

There are two types of expectations:
1. Learning expectations
2. Social/organizational expectations

It is important to concentrate on expectations that affect your students' learning outcomes. Let's take a moment to discuss both.

LEARNING EXPECTATION

I once had a student in my graduate class who had very simple expectations in her classroom. She used the mnemonic DEAR.

    D   Discover how you learn best

How to Avoid Conflicts BEFORE Your Class is Disrupted

- E   Evaluate all work
- A   Apply effort to all your work
- R   Respect the learning environment of others

All of the above expectations are main topics and can be discussed at great lengths.

However, the mnemonic is easy to recall and is a terrific reminder to your students as to what is expected of them in your classroom. In fact, my student brought food into her classroom and actually had a feast while discussing the class expectations!

Is this a simple and terrific way to make a learning connection? Absolutely!

SOCIAL AND ORGANIZATION EXPECTATIONS

These are the expectations which have no learning outcomes but are necessary to keep chaos from occurring in your room. It is a good idea to combine these expectations into the learning list.

For example, when you tell the children to "apply effort" that means coming prepared to class or being in your seat when the bell rings. When you tell your students to "respect the learning environment," that could mean or not talking when others are talking.

Following, you will find five suggestions that will help you combine your learning expectations with your social/organization expectations.

1. KEEP YOUR LIST OF EXPECTATIONS VISIBLE IN THE ROOM

Creating Classroom Expectations

Actually, it would be better to post TWO lists of expectations in your room...one in the front and one in the back. This way there is a gentle reminder of your expectations no matter where your students are seated.

This teacher who used FEAST in her room printed the word on the top of all handouts she passed out to her students. She never gave the students an opportunity to forget the importance of having expectations in her room and making sure they followed them.

2. KEEP YOUR EXPECTATION LIST SHORT

Choose no more than FIVE rules for each type. It is very difficult to remember more than FIVE.

I did a presentation at a high school on building communications with students. Having the school handbook on my podium, I asked the teachers to write the school expectations down on a piece of paper. There were 19 expectations!

All of the teachers did not remember them. Because your list will be short....CHOOSE WISELY!

3. STATE EXPECTATIONS POSITIVELY

If I said to you...close your eyes and do NOT picture a pink elephant. What do you see in your mind's eye? Exactly! A pink elephant. Your brain has a hard time processing the word NOT. Therefore, you processed my request as...picture a pink elephant. Which is what you did!

When you tell a student NOT to run, of course, the student runs!!!! Instead of saying "no talking when we work independently" state it "we will be quiet when the class works independently.

4. FOCUS ON OBSERVABLE BEHAVIORS

Tell the students what the expectation "feels like, looks like, and sounds like." Make sure they can be described as physical behaviors. By doing so, you are activating emotions. Using emotions in a learning experience helps connection information to long term memory.

5. USE KEY WORDS THAT CAN BE IDENTIFIED

Highlight, underline or write in italics the words that identify successful learning behaviors. Doing so emphasizes the helps trigger retention of the behaviors expected.

It is important to give students the kind of rules they need and want. On the next page is a chart showing the types of rules different types of learners prefer:

LEARNING STYLES CHART

Kinesthetic Learners:

Creating Classroom Expectations

- Expectations that tell them WHAT they can do
- Expectations that tell them WHEN they can do it
- Expectations that ask for competence and skill
- Expectations that support interaction with other such as "Help each other learn"

Auditory Learners:

- Enjoy creating expectations
- Enjoy how discussing expectations are working now and in the future
- Enjoy expectations that encourage conversation such as "Listen to others"

Visual Learners:

- Like to study the expectations
- Like to evaluate the expectations
- Will support an expectation it they "see" it working
- Support "visual" expectations such as "look for quality in your work."

Just as you need to teach math facts or scientific theories, it is important for you to "teach" rules. Spend time discussing them. You students will get the message that classroom rules are important since you are taking valuable time out of the day for this discussion. And don't stop there once the discussion is over.

How to Avoid Conflicts BEFORE Your Class is Disrupted

Design lesson plans to teach the rules. For example, ask your students to either create a drawing depicting the classroom rules, present a skit or a puppet show with the classroom rules, or present a speech on the rules and consequences of breaking the rules will be. Notice the same assessment...three different ways that depict three different learning styles.

As with any learning objective, reinforcement is necessary. Reviewing expectations result in a recommitment to them. When is it necessary to review?

- When a new student comes into your classroom
- When your students have broken your expectation
- When something positive occurred because an expectation was followed.

Remember, praise goes a long way in making sure your room runs smoothly and you are "leaving no child behind."

LISTENING TO CONCERNS ACTIVITY

Creating Classroom Expectations

On a piece of paper, create a table similar to the one below. List 10 the major activities you use in your classroom. Decide what predominate learning style was used. Ex. skits are kinesthetic, reading a book is visual, lecturing is auditory. Tally the number of activities by style to discover is you favored a particular style over the others.

Activity   Learning Styles

Activity	Learning Styles

Tally
Auditory _____
Visual _____
Kinesthetic_____

4

Following Classroom Expectations

In the last chapter, we talked about the definition of "expectations." In this lesson, we will discuss the importance of presenting classroom expectations in a way that is processed easily for each individual learning style.

The expectations you feel are the ones appropriate and needed for you to conduct a "thinking" classroom are processed and learned differently by your students.

As you know by now, the reason being everyone has a different learning style. I can't emphasis enough to you how important it is for you to remember that and not let frustration sink in when a student doesn't quite "get it."

Following Classroom Expectations

Take a breath and try presenting a different way.

Let's get on with getting your students to follow your expectations. As every teacher knows, students decide if they are going to follow or not follow classroom procedures and expectations.

Also, as every teacher knows, the way they do that is to test the consequences of their behavior.

The question here is...how does the student "test?"

Learning styles follow the same general procedure when making behavioral decisions...they collect information. It is how the information is collected that is different. At this point, it seems the auditory and visual learners are usually easier to manage when collecting information before making those decisions since they generally do not use movement.

This is another clue you are not dealing with a kinesthetic child as you will see in a moment.

COLLECTING INFORMATION BY LEARNING STYLES

KINESTHETIC STUDENTS will experiment with classroom expectations. They will break the expectations and see what the consequences will be or if there actually be any consequences. This is the time you must be very clear of what will happen and completely follow through. Because of the way a kinesthetic student's approach to classroom management, he is the student who seems to be disciplined more often. This is the child who is constantly accused of "acting WITHOUT thinking. I want you to think of that child differently...he is "acting in order TO think!"

AUDITORY STUDENTS will talk about the classroom expectations. This is how they collect the information about the expectations and think out the consequences. They will engage you in lengthy conversations or seem to ask "thousands" of questions. All they are doing is making sure they have all the facts correct and they are will make the "right" decision.

VISUAL STUDENTS will watch, study and read the expectations. They are very slow to make up their mind before making a decision on classroom behavior. A visual learner doesn't like to discuss what is going on in his mind before he has made a decision. However, don't mistake quietness for lack of attention. This student is very awareness of what is going on in the room. He is just watching, waiting and deciding privately.

WHEN THE DECISION IS MADE BY THE STUDENT TO FOLLOW CLASSROOM EXPECTATIONS

Because classroom expectations are interpreted differently by the various learning styles, it is important to be as specific as you can when a specific expectation is presented to your students.

Let's try something. I would like to you get a piece of paper and pencil. I am going to ask you to write how you would interpret the following:

- A STUDENT PUTTING FORTH EFFORT

Following Classroom Expectations

- A STUDENT SUPPORTING CLASSMATES DURING A LEARNING EPISODE
- A STUDENT THINKING CREATIVELY.

Now, let's look at how the different styles would interpret those statements. See if what you wrote matches the needs list on the next page.

NEEDS LIST

PUT FORTH EFFORT
- A kinesthetic learner would need to be doing something
- A visual learner would need a degree of quiet concentration
- An auditory learner would talk through the learning objective

SUPPORT CLASSMATES DURING A LEARNING EPISODE
- A kinesthetic learner would help a classmate create or do something
- A visual learner would help a classmate by letting him have quiet time to reflect on the learning
- An auditory learner would help a classmate by discussing an talking him through the learning

THINK CREATIVELY

- A kinesthetic learner would need to create or invent something

- A visual learner would silently visual a situation which would more than likely end with a visual representation of the thinking
- An auditory learner likes to brainstorm with other students

It is easy for you to understand how there are quite significant differences between interpretations of the statements. This is why is it extremely important for you to be specific in what you expect from your students. Leave no room for individuals to translate the expectations into their learning style.

RESISTING THE EXPECTATIONS

I have heard quite often teachers asking, "Why don't some of my students follow the rules in the classroom." The answer to that question is, at this point, quite obvious. With the assumption the expectations are clear and understood by all your students, they may not choose to follow them because of individual learning preferences.

Let's take a look at some reasons for resistance:

KINESTHETIC LEARNERS resist expectations because the rules may be:
- Restricting -
- Lacking freedom of movement
- Be written in a form of "what not to do"

A kinesthetic learner shows resistance by "physically acting out."

Following Classroom Expectations

VISUAL LEARNERS resist expectations because the rules may be:

- Not open to discussion
- Restrict ability to talk unless there is a verbal outlet

A visual learner shows resistance by challenging the expectation so a discussion can begin.

AUDITORY LEARNERS resist expectations because the rules may be:

- Not "workable" (They will be able to tell you why when asked. Listen carefully. You may discover an alternative expectation that is very doable in your classroom)

An Auditory learner shows resistance by sitting with an angry looks on their face and not participating. They are quite good at passive-aggressive behavior.

Please be patient when you are presenting classroom expectations. Even if you were careful to discuss your expectations in a multi-sensory way and thoroughly explained the benefits of each expectation, every learning style needs time "digest" them in their own way. The general time frame for the class to fully follow expectations and completely accept them without challenge is about 4-6 weeks.

Choosing Consequences
===

5

Choosing Consequences

At this time, you know so much about learning styles and how they react to expectations in the classroom. Let's tie this information to actually creating a discipline plan for your classroom.

By creating and establishing classroom expectations, the learning behaviors should be followed by all students. Your reaction to a student who breaks the expectation can determine if the issue is resolved amicably or cause additional confrontation.

This is why the teacher really needs to understand learning styles. Then and only then, does the teacher understand the importance of honoring the student and helping the student keep his/dignity in the face of adversity,

LET'S LOOK AT THE KINESTHETIC STUDENT

Choosing Consequences

The kinesthetic learner learns through experimenting. So it shouldn't come to the surprise of his teacher when this student breaks the rules by testing the limits. Because this student learns well through physical movement, moving close to him when giving a warning makes a physical statement. Remember to keep a normal level voice and also to keep your body language relaxed. A kinesthetic responds to reminders of past experiences. Therefore, just saying something as simple as, "John, remember what happened when you didn't do your work last week" can have a positive effect on John's work.

LET'S LOOK AT THE VISUAL STUDENT

It is important to have this type of learner look at you. Just walk into her line of vision BEFORE you begin talking. Your words are not as powerful as your presence. It is much more effective showing her what you want. Example...point to the expectation poster. Another good strategy is to have color coded behavior cards. A red card can be inappropriate behavior and blue card can be for appropriate behavior. You can simply slip one of these cards on the desk or into the hands of a visual student. Please try not to let others see you do this. It is not our goal to embarrass. If you are uncomfortable with color coded cards, just handing a note for the student to read may be an alternative.

LET'S LOOK AT THE AUDITORY STUDENT

The auditory student responds to a simple strategy...reprimand should be firmly delivered with an explanation. In fact, this style responds to an explanation better than any other style. Remember an auditory learner is quite sensitive to change in pitch and tone. Therefore, you should practice your delivery. Keep your tone neutral and confident. Make sure your delivery is not perceived as threatening or impatient.

HOW TO MATCH CONSEQUENCES TO LEARNING STYLES

The problem with discipline many classrooms seem to have a "one size fits all" policy. It is important to remember that all students do not respond equally to that "one size" policy. A time out may be very effective to one student who sees it as a negative experience and be a reward to another since the time out may be seen as a break from classroom.

It stands to reason...if teachers plan their lessons to meet the needs of different learning styles...the discipline policy of the classroom will have various consequences to the same "offense" with the choice option. That choice option will be determined by you!

Let's take this concept further. For each expectation, give your students a list of possible consequences. For example, a consequence for breaking a rule may include a time out, a letter to the parent, losing the privilege.

The consequence of following an expectation may include more free time, a certificate, and a special privilege. Also, explain that all students will follow the same expectations and there will be consequences for breaking or following them. However, they will not know beforehand what the consequences will be. Do you see how effective this can be?

NEGATIVE CONSEQUENCES

Choosing Consequences

It is not our desire to punish when "dishing out" negative consequences. It is our purpose to encourage our students to have personal responsibility. A negative consequence serves as a deterrent.

I remember a friend of mine wanting to lose weight. Candy was tough for her not to eat. So, she wore an elastic band on her wrist. Whenever she ate chocolate, she snapped the elastic. Obviously, it hurt her! She then connected the pain with chocolate. After awhile she didn't have to snap the band...just looking at chocolate reminded her of pain. Thus, she stopped eating chocolate!

Keep this story in mind. This is exactly what we are trying to do in the classroom. The negative consequence is to serve as an "I don't want to experience this again so I won't do it" attitude.

Let's look at what the various learning styles truly consider negative and how you can bring them into your classroom.

KINESTHETIC

These students want to avoid physical consequences such as being moved to another seat, a time out, doing a repetitive activity (cleaning off desks for example), and isolation

AUDITORY

These students want to avoid being reprimanded verbally, being restricted on talking, verbal apologies.

VISUAL

How to Avoid Conflicts BEFORE Your Class is Disrupted

This learner wants to avoid being singled out or being watched by others. A simple identification of them and their misbehavior may be a strong deterrent. Another strong deterrent is moving them to the front of the room or making the consequence visible to others.

As a sidebar...I am not a strong fan of negative consequences. I really believe that if the learning needs of students are met by the teacher's lessons which include activities for everyone, negative consequences will no longer be necessary.

POSITIVE CONSEQUENCES

There should be as many or more positive consequences as negative ones. Students tend to gravitate to the positive consequences that meet their learning style needs. Visuals will love more time to read. Kinesthetics will love more outside time. Auditories will love more time to talk with classmates.

KINESTHETIC

A kinesthetic enjoys physical rewards and activities. They love being the first to leave the classroom or the first in line. Giving stickers, toys, pencils, allowing them to lead an activity (ex flag salute), writing on the board, choose where to sit are all examples of consequences appreciated by this style.

AUDITORY

An auditory learner will respond extremely well when there is verbal recognition and approval. As a reward, they love to have time when they can socialize with their friends...they love to talk! Giving a certificate as a reward is also important to an auditory. By showing or displaying the certificate, a discussion about it will begin.

VISUAL

A visual learner likes any type of reward that can be seen by him or others. A written note, a certificate of achievement, stickers, stars and prizes are appreciated by the visual learner.

Activity

How to Avoid Conflicts BEFORE Your Class is Disrupted

On a separate sheet of paper, list all the "rules" or expectations you have in your classroom. Choose two consequences you could attach to each rule. Decide which consequence you will use first or second.

Postscript

Hopefully, using the information in this book will give your lesson planning a new perspective. Planning a lesson keeping, not only keeping the end result but discipline strategies in mind, may help reach all your students.

After all, isn't it an educator's goal to...

ACTIVATE THE POTENTIAL OF EVERY STUDENT!

www.ingramcontent.com/pod-product-compliance
Lightning Source LLC
Chambersburg PA
CBHW071801040426
42446CB00012B/2652